Y0-AWG-332

Freestyle Instant Pot Cookbook 2018

The Ultimate Freestyle Instant Pot Cookbook 2018

Jessica Houck

TABLE OF CONTENTS

WEIGHT WATCHERS FREESTYLE BREAKFAST RECIPES

PEACHES AND CREAM OATMEAL

SERVING SIZE: 1
SERVINGS PER RECIPE: 8
FREESTYLE POINTS PER SERVING: 2
CALORIES: 234
COOKING TIME: 10 MINUTES
INGREDIENTS:

Old-fashioned oats—4 cups

Water—3 ½ cups

Milk—3 ½ cups

Salt—1 teaspoon

Ground cinnamon—1 teaspoon

Sugar—$^1/_3$ cup

Peaches—4

NUTRITION INFORMATION:

Carbohydrate—42 g

Protein—12 g

Fat—6g

Sodium—45 mg

Cholesterol—5 mg

INSTRUCTIONS:

1. First of all, wash the peaches well. Start peeling and then chopping them. Keep some slices for garnishing later on.

2. Make the Instant Pot ready and put all the ingredients in it. Stir well.

3. Close the lid of the Instant Pot and let it cook for about 6 minutes on the Multigrain option.

4. Once it has finished cooking, put sugar, milk, brown sugar, cream, and the sliced peaches in it.

5. Your dish is ready to be served.

RICE PUDDING

SERVING SIZE: 1
SERVINGS PER RECIPE: 4
FREESTYLE POINTS PER SERVING: 1
CALORIES: 156
COOKING TIME: 35 MINUTES

INGREDIENTS:

Short-grain brown rice—1 cup

Water—1 ½ cups

Vanilla extract—1 tablespoon

Cinnamon stick—1

Butter—1 tablespoon

Raisins—1 cup

Honey—3 tablespoons

Heavy cream—½ cup

NUTRITION INFORMATION:

Carbohydrate—23g

Protein—34g

Fat—2 g

Sodium—567 mg

Cholesterol—24 mg

INSTRUCTIONS:

1. Take the Instant Pot and add rice, water, cinnamon stick, vanilla extract, and butter in it. Close the lid of the Instant Pot.

2. Select the Manual button and set the time to 20 minutes.

3. Allow for natural release of pressure.

4. Take out the cinnamon stick from the Instant Pot and discard it.

5. Add honey, raisins, and cream in the pot.

6. Select the Sauté button and select the temperature to low heat. Let it simmer for about 5 minutes.

7. Your dish is ready to be served.

BACON RANCH POTATOES

SERVING SIZE: 1
SERVINGS PER RECIPE: 6
FREESTYLE POINTS PER SERVING: 3
CALORIES: 237
COOKING TIME: 15 MINUTES

INGREDIENTS:

Red potatoes—2 pounds, 1 kilogram, scrubbed

Bacon strips—3

Dried parsley—2 teaspoons

Kosher salt—1 teaspoon

Garlic powder—1 teaspoon

Cheddar cheese—4 ounces, shredded

Ranch dressing—$^1/_3$ cup

NUTRITION INFORMATION:

Carbohydrate—62g

Protein—34 g

Fat—4 g

Sodium—72 mg

Cholesterol—25 mg

INSTRUCTIONS:

1. First, cut the potatoes into 1-inch sized pieces.

2. Now chop the bacon into small pieces.

3. Take the Instant Pot and set it on Sauté mode. Now add the bacon in it and let it cook until crispy.

4. Put the potatoes in it along with garlic powder, salt,and dried parsley.

5. Pour $^1/_3$ cup of water in it.

6. Set the Instant Pot on manual high pressure for about 7 minutes.

7. Once it has finished cooking, do a quick release of pressure. Open the lid carefully.

8. Put the ranch dressing and cheese in it. Mix well.

9. Your dish is ready to be served.

BREAKFAST QUINOA

SERVING SIZE: 1
SERVINGS PER RECIPE: 6
FREESTYLE POINTS PER SERVING: 2
CALORIES: 135
COOKING TIME: 1 MINUTE

INGREDIENTS:

Quinoa—1 ½ cups, well rinsed

Water—2 ¼ cups

Maple syrup—2 tablespoons

Vanilla—½ teaspoon

Ground cinnamon—¼ teaspoon

Salt—to taste

FOR GARNISHING:

Milk

Fresh berries

Sliced almonds

NUTRITION INFORMATION:

Carbohydrate—45g

Protein—8 g

Fat—5 g

Sodium—275mg

Cholesterol—24mg

INSTRUCTIONS:

1. Take the Instant Pot and add the water and quinoa in it. Put vanilla, maple syrup, cinnamon, and salt in it.

2. Press the High Pressure button and allow it to cook it for about a minute or two. Once the Instant Pot turns off, let it rest for about 10 minutes.

3. Allow for a quick release of pressure. Remove the lid from the Instant Pot.

4. With the help of a fork, fluff the quinoa well.

5. Add hot milk on top of it and garnish it with sliced almonds and fresh berries.

6. Your dish is ready to be served.

APPLE BREAD WITH SALTED CARAMEL

SERVING SIZE: 1
SERVINGS PER RECIPE: 10
FREESTYLE POINTS PER SERVING: 1
CALORIES: 551
COOKING TIME: 1 HOUR AND 10 MINUTES

INGREDIENTS:

Apples—3 cups, peeled, cored, and cubed

Sugar—1 cup

Eggs—2

Vanilla—1 tablespoon

Apple pie spice—1 tablespoon

Flour—2 cups

Butter stick—1

Baking powder—1 tablespoon

FOR TOPPING:

Salted butter stick—1

Brown sugar—2 cups

Heavy cream—1 cup

Powdered sugar—2 cups

NUTRITION INFORMATION:

Carbohydrate—113 g

Protein—4 g

Fat—10 g

Sodium—38 mg

Cholesterol—65 mg

INSTRUCTIONS:

1. Take a mixer and add butter, eggs, sugar, and apple pie spice in it. Blend it well until it turns smooth and creamy.

2. Add the apples in the mixture. Stir well.

3. Take another bowl and add baking powder and flour in it. Whisk it well.

4. Add this dry mixture to the wet mixture half at a time.

5. Once the batter turns thick and has gained a good consistency, pour it into a springform pan.

6. Take the Instant Pot and add a trivet in it. Add a cup of water to the bottom of the pan.

7. Now place the pan on the trivet inside the Instant Pot.

8. Select manual high pressure and let it cook for about 70 minutes.

9. Meanwhile, to prepare the icing, take a small saucepan. Put some brown sugar in it and let it melt for about 3 minutes. Once the sugar has melted, add the heavy cream in it and let it cook for about 2 minutes. The moment it starts thickening, remove it from the heat and allow it to cool. Add the powdered sugar and whisk it well.

10. Do a quick release of pressure from the Instant Pot.

11. Remove the springform pan from the Instant Pot and add the icing on the top of it. Your dish is ready to be served.

SOY YOGURT

SERVING SIZE: 1
SERVINGS PER RECIPE: 4
FREESTYLE POINTS PER SERVING: 7
CALORIES: 111
COOKING TIME: 14 HOURS

INGREDIENTS:

Soy milk—1 box, 32 ounces

Vegan plain yogurt—2 tablespoons

NUTRITION INFORMATION:

Carbohydrate—45g

Protein—23 g

Fat—3 g

Sodium—391 mg

Cholesterol—154 mg

INSTRUCTIONS:

1. Take two wide mouth pint jars and divide the soy milk between them.

2. Put a tablespoon of yogurt in each jar. Stir well.

3. Make your Instant Pot ready and place the jars at the bottom of it.

4. Close the lid of the Instant Pot and make sure the vent is sealed. Select the Yogurt option. Let it set for about 14 hours.

5. Before serving, stir the soy yogurt well. Consume it within 5 days if refrigerated. Your dish is ready to be served.

TWICE-BAKED POTATOES CASSEROLE

SERVING SIZE: 1
SERVINGS PER RECIPE: 6
FREESTYLE POINTS PER SERVING: 8
CALORIES: 424
COOKING TIME: 20 MINUTES

INGREDIENTS:

Potatoes—5 pounds

Butter stick—1 ½

Salt—to taste

Pepper—to taste

Milk—1 cup

Sour cream—1 cup

Ranch seasoning mix—1

Shredded cheese—2 cups

Green onions—1 bundle, chopped

Bacon slices—4, cooked and crumbled

NUTRITION INFORMATION:

Carbohydrate—32 g

Protein—13 g

Fat—27 g

Sodium—581 mg

Cholesterol—74 mg

INSTRUCTIONS:

1. Cut the potatoes along with the skin into chunk-sized pieces.

2. Take the Instant Pot and place the potatoes in it. Pour a cup of water in it. Put the stick butter in it and season it with salt and pepper.

3. Put the lid of the Instant Pot and make sure the valve is in the sealing position.

4. Select the Manual button and set the time to about 6 minutes.

5. Let it cook until it beeps.

6. Once finished cooking, do a quick release of pressure.

7. Now add some more butter and milk in it.

8. With the help of a hand electric masher, mash everything inside the Instant Pot.

9. Pour the sour cream along with the ranch seasoning dressing in it. Mix them well.

10. Stir in the shredded cheese along with the green onions.

11. Take a baking dish and place the mixture into it.

12. Sprinkle the remaining cheese, bacon, and chives all over it.

13. Let it bake for about 350°F in the oven for about 20 minutes.

14. Your dish is ready to be served.

BACON AND EGG RISOTTO

SERVING SIZE: 1
SERVINGS PER RECIPE: 2
FREESTYLE POINTS PER SERVING: 4
CALORIES: 292
COOKING TIME: 10 MINUTES

INGREDIENTS:

Bacon slices—3, center cut, chopped

Onion—1/3 cup, chopped

Arborio rice—¾ cup

Dry white wine—3 tablespoons

Chicken broth—1 ½ cups

Eggs—2

Parmesan cheese—2 tablespoons, grated

Salt—to taste

Pepper—to taste

Chives—for garnishing

NUTRITION INFORMATION:

Carbohydrate—16 g

Protein—12 g

Fat—11 g

Sodium—959 mg

Cholesterol—0 mg

INSTRUCTIONS:

1. Take the Instant Pot and select the Sauté mode.

2. Put the bacon in it and let it cook until the fat begins to render. Let it cook for about 5 minutes until the bacon turns crispy.

3. Now add the onions in it and let it cook for about 3 minutes. Add the rice in it and stir well. Let it sauté for about a minute.

4. Pour the dry white wine and stir it in the Instant Pot. Scrape out any brown bits from the bottom of the pan.

5. Let the wine absorb well. Pour the chicken broth in it and stir well. Put the lid on of the Instant Pot.

6. Seal the valve of the Instant Pot and select the Manual mode. Let it cook for about 5 minutes.

7. When the rice has finished cooking, cook the eggs according to your choice.

8. Do a natural release of pressure and open the lid of the Instant Pot.

9. Add the Parmesan cheese in it and sprinkle salt and pepper as desired. Stir well.

10. Divide the rice between two plates, top it with the cooked egg, and garnish it with chopped chives.

11. Your dish is ready to be served.

GREEN CHILI TACOS

SERVING SIZE: 1
SERVINGS PER RECIPE: 4
FREESTYLE POINTS PER SERVING: 4
CALORIES: 155
COOKING TIME: 2 HOURS

INGREDIENTS:

FOR THE GREEN CHILI:

- Pork shoulder—2 pounds
- Chicken broth—¾ cup
- Roasted crushed tomatoes—1 can, 14 ounces
- Green chilies—2 mild hatch
- Green chilies—2 hot hatch
- Onion—1, chopped
- Lard or bacon fat—3 tablespoons
- Cumin—1 ½ teaspoons
- Salt—to taste
- Pepper—to taste

FOR THE BREAKFAST TACOS:

- Green chili—8 ounces
- Eggs—3, scrambled
- Tortillas—2

FOR GARNISHING:

- Sliced avocado
- Mayo
- Cilantro
- Lime wedges

NUTRITION INFORMATION:

Carbohydrate—38g

Protein—31 g

Fat—9 g

Sodium—511 mg

Cholesterol—23 mg

INSTRUCTIONS:

1. Take a dish and place the pork shoulder on it. Season it well with cumin, salt, and pepper. Set it aside.

2. Make the Instant Pot ready and put the lard in it. Melt the lard on Sauté mode high heat setting.

3. After the lard has melted, add the onions in it. Sauté it until brown and caramelized.

4. Now sear the pork in it from all the sides inside the Instant Pot. Make sure you get a nice crust of the pork. Take out the pork from the Instant Pot.

5. To deglaze, scrape out any brown bits from the bottom of the Instant Pot.

6. Put the green chilies, diced tomatoes, and the pork in it. Close the lid of the Instant Pot and let it cook on Manual mode and high pressure for about 90 minutes.

7. Once finished cooking, go for a quick release of pressure.

8. Shred the pork with the help of two forks.

9. To prepare the breakfast tacos, first of all, heat a skillet over medium heat. Put the green chilies in it and reheat it.

10. Take the tortillas and add the green chilies and scrambled eggs in it. Add crispy pork in it and garnish it with mayo, sliced avocado, cilantro, and lime juice from the lime wedge.

11. Your dish is ready to be served.

EGGS EN COCOTTE

SERVING SIZE: 1
SERVINGS PER RECIPE: 3
FREESTYLE POINTS PER SERVING: 2
CALORIES: 257
COOKING TIME: 2 MINUTES

INGREDIENTS:

Cream—3 tablespoons

Fresh pasture-raised eggs—3

Chives—1 tablespoon

Salt—to taste

Black pepper—to taste

Water—1 cup

Butter, room temperature—as required

NUTRITION INFORMATION:

Carbohydrate—42g

Protein—24g

Fat—31 g

Sodium—21 mg

Cholesterol—36 mg

INSTRUCTIONS:

1. Take three ramekins and wipe it well with the butter.

2. Add 1 tablespoon of the cream into each ramekin.

3. Crack the eggs along with the yolk intact inside each ramekin.

4. Season it with chives.

5. Make the Instant Pot ready and place a rack inside the Instant Pot.

6. Pour a cup of water at the bottom of the pot. Now place the ramekins on the rack.

7. Close the lid of the pot and make sure the valve is in the sealing position.

8. Select the Manual button and let it cook for about 2 minutes.

9. Press the Pressure Cook option and allow it to cook on low heat.

10. Once the timer beeps after 2 minutes, do a quick release of pressure.

11. Sprinkle salt and pepper as desired.

12. Your dish is ready to be served.

CRUSTLESS SHRIMP AND SPINACH QUICHE

SERVING SIZE: 1
SERVINGS PER RECIPE: 4
FREESTYLE POINTS PER SERVING: 9
CALORIES: 395
COOKING TIME: 50 MINUTES

INGREDIENTS:

Eggs—4

Half-and-half—1 cup

Salt—½–1 teaspoon

Sweet smoked paprika—1 teaspoon

Herbes de Provence—1 teaspoon

Parmesan or Swiss cheese—1 cup, shredded

Green onions—1 cup, chopped, green and white parts

Shrimp meat—8 ounces

Spinach—3 cups

NUTRITION INFORMATION:

Carbohydrate—19 g

Protein—22 g

Fat—25 g

Sodium—526 mg

Cholesterol—236 mg

INSTRUCTIONS:

1. In a large bowl, put eggs in it along with the half-and-half. Whisk it well.

2. Sprinkle Herbes de Provence, salt, black pepper, sweet smoked paprika, and shredded cheese in it. Mix it well.

3. Put the chopped green onions and the shrimp meat in it.

4. Add the spinach over it.

5. Cover the springform pan with a bigger sized aluminum sheet and crimp it at the bottom.

6. Pour the egg mixture in the pan. Cover it loosely with the foil.

7. Add two cups of water in the Instant Pot. Place a steamer rack inside the Instant Pot.

8. Now place the springform pan on the trivet inside the Instant Pot.

9. Let it cook on high pressure for about 40 minutes. Once done, allow it to sit for about 10 minutes.

10. Once finished cooking, do a quick release of pressure.

11. Take out the hot silicone pan carefully from the pot.

12. Take a knife and slowly loosen the edges of the shrimp quiche from the pan.

13. Remove it from the pan and plate it.

14. Your dish is ready to be served.

MINI CHICKEN QUICHE

SERVING SIZE: 1
SERVINGS PER RECIPE: 6
FREESTYLE POINTS PER SERVING: 3
CALORIES: 160
COOKING TIME: 5 MINUTES

INGREDIENTS:

Swiss cheese—3 ounces, shredded

Chicken—2 ounces, chopped into bite-sized pieces

Scallion—1, chopped

Eggs—4

Heavy cream half-and-half—¼ cup

Sea salt—½ teaspoon

Water—1 cup

NUTRITION INFORMATION:

Carbohydrate—3 g

Protein—8 g

Fat—3 g

Sodium—267 mg

Cholesterol—15 mg

INSTRUCTIONS:

1. First, take the silicone mold and put Swiss cheese in it.

2. Press the cheese inside the mold to make the sides slightly up.

3. Now divide the chicken pieces evenly and place it on top of the cheese.

4. Sprinkle chopped scallions.

5. Beat the egg along with salt and cream in the hand blender. Also, add the cheese and the chicken mixture in it. Blend it well.

6. Pour 1 cup of water inside the Instant Pot. Put a trivet inside it. Place the silicone mold containing the chicken and cheese mixture on top of the trivet.

7. Close the lid of the Instant Pot. Make sure the valve is in a sealing position.

8. Let it cook on high pressure for about 5 minutes.

9. Once finished cooking, you will hear a beep sound. Allow it to sit for about 5 minutes.

10. Do a quick release of pressure.

11. Flip the silicone tray on the plate to place the mini chicken quiche. Carefully turn the mini chicken quiche over to keep the cooked chicken pieces intact on top of cheese crust.

12. Your dish is ready to be served.

NUTELLA QUINOA

SERVING SIZE: 1
SERVINGS PER RECIPE: 5
FREESTYLE POINTS PER SERVING: 2
CALORIES: 240
COOKING TIME: 10 MINUTES

INGREDIENTS:

Butter—1 teaspoon

Quinoa—1 cup

Coconut milk—1 can

Milk—$1/3$ cup

Cocoa powder—1 tablespoon

Hazelnut extract—½ teaspoon

Maple syrup—1–2 teaspoons

NUTRITION INFORMATION:

Carbohydrate—23 g

Protein—5 g

Fat—15 g

Sodium—16 mg

Cholesterol—1 mg

INSTRUCTIONS:

1. Make the Instant Pot ready and select the Sauté option.

2. Add the butter in it and allow it to melt.

3. Add the quinoa in it and mix it well. Stir frequently while you sauté the quinoa for about 10 minutes. Toast it well.

4. Keep the Instant Pot on the Sauté mode. Put the other ingredients in the Instant Pot and stir them together.

5. Allow it to cook for about a minute. Make sure the cocoa powder starts getting fully combined in the mixture.

6. Keep the Instant Pot on the Warm mode. Select the manual setting to increase it to high pressure.

7. Set the timer for about 2 minutes. Make sure the Instant Pot is in a sealing position.

8. Allow it to cook for about 5 minutes. Let it first rest for about 5 minutes. Do a quick release of pressure.

9. Carefully open the lid of the Instant Pot.

10. Divide the Nutella quinoa into serving bowls.

11. Garnish it with nuts, fresh fruits, coconuts, etc.

12. Your dish is ready to be served.

WEIGHT WATCHERS
FREESTYLE LUNCH RECIPES

CILANTRO LIME RICE

SERVING SIZE: 1
SERVINGS PER RECIPE: 8
FREESTYLE POINTS PER SERVING: 2
CALORIES: 157
COOKING TIME: 17 MINUTES

INGREDIENTS:

Vegetable broth—1 can, 14 ounces

Water—¾ cup

Canola oil—2 tablespoons

Lime juice—3 tablespoons, divided

White rice—2 cups, long grain

Lime zest—1 lime

Cilantro—½ cup, freshly chopped

Salt—½ teaspoon

NUTRITION INFORMATION:

Carbohydrate—25 g

Protein—16 g

Fat—8 g

Sodium—453 mg

Cholesterol—12 mg

INSTRUCTIONS:

1. Make the Instant Pot ready and pour the vegetable broth in it. Add some water in it along with canola oil. Put the rice in the Instant Pot and add 2 tablespoons of the lime juice in it.

2. Close the lid of the Instant Pot and press the Rice button. Allow the rice to cook for about 12 minutes.

3. Once the rice has finished cooking, let the rice sit for about 5 minutes.

4. After 5 minutes, go for a quick release of pressure. Remove the lid of the Instant Pot.

5. Transfer the rice in a large bowl. With the help of a fork, fluff the rice and put another tablespoon of the lime juice in the Instant Pot. Also, add the lime zest and sprinkle salt as desired.

6. Garnish it with chopped cilantro and fluff the rice again.

7. Your dish is ready to be served.

GUINNESS LAMB SHANKS

SERVING SIZE: 1
SERVINGS PER RECIPE: 4
FREESTYLE POINTS PER SERVING: 5
CALORIES: 218
COOKING TIME: 2 HOURS

INGREDIENTS:

Olive oil—1 teaspoon

Lamb shanks—4, 1.25 kilograms

Leek—1, trimmed, thinly sliced

Carrots—2, diced

Garlic cloves—2, thinly sliced

Tomato paste—2 tablespoons

Beef stock—2 cups

Guinness beer—1 cup

Mashed potato

Steamed green beans

NUTRITION INFORMATION:

Carbohydrate—31g

Protein—57 g

Fat—14 g

Sodium—1,132 mg

Cholesterol—146 mg

INSTRUCTIONS:

1. In a large frying pan, put some oil. Heat the oil over medium-high heat.

2. Season the lamb with salt and black pepper. Put the lamb in the pan. Allow it to cook for about 6 minutes. Turn it frequently to make sure the lamb is thoroughly cooked through. Let the lamb brown from all the sides. Transfer everything to the Instant Pot.

3. Now adjust the heat to medium-high heat and add carrot and leek in it. Let it cook for about 5 minutes until it turns tender. Add garlic in it and let it cook for about a minute until it turns fragrant.

4. Add tomato paste in the Instant Pot and cook it for approximately 30 minutes. Stir it well. Add the stock and the Guinness in the Instant Pot. Season it with salt and pepper.

5. Pour the mixture all over the lamb and close the lid of the Instant Pot. Allow it to cook for about an hour until the lamb turns tender.

6. Transfer everything to a bowl.

7. First, plate the lamb shanks along with the bread and mashed potatoes. Also, add the green beans on the side.

8. Your dish is ready to be served.

ETHIOPIAN SPINACH AND LENTIL SOUP

SERVING SIZE: 1
SERVINGS PER RECIPE: 4
FREESTYLE POINTS PER SERVING: 3
CALORIES: 449
COOKING TIME: 10 MINUTES

INGREDIENTS:

Unsalted butter—2 tablespoons

Olive oil—1 tablespoon

Red onion—1, medium, finely chopped

Garlic powder—1 teaspoon

Ground coriander—2 teaspoons

Cinnamon powder—½ teaspoon

Turmeric powder—½ teaspoon

Clove powder—¼ teaspoon

Cayenne pepper—¼ teaspoon

Cardamom powder—¼ teaspoon

Nutmeg—¼ teaspoon, freshly grated

Brown lentils—2 cups

Water—8 cups

Salt—2 teaspoons

Pepper—¼ teaspoon

Fresh spinach—6 ounces, 4 packed cups

Lemon juice—4 tablespoons

NUTRITION INFORMATION:

Carbohydrate—67 g

Protein—25 g

Fat—11 g

Sodium—1,214 mg

Cholesterol—15 mg

INSTRUCTIONS:

1. Take the Instant Pot and select the Sauté mode. Add butter in it and once it has melted, add oil, onion, garlic, cinnamon, clove, cardamom, turmeric, nutmeg, cayenne, and coriander in it. Sauté everything together for about 3 minutes.

2. Pour water in the Instant Pot and put the lentils in it.

3. Close the lid of the Instant Pot and allow it to cook for about 10 minutes. Cook on high pressure.

4. Once it has finished cooking, do a natural release of pressure for nearly about 15 minutes.

5. Take off the lid of the Instant Pot and sprinkle salt and black pepper as desired.

6. Put the spinach leaves in it and allow it to cook. Let the spinach leaves wilt inside the soup.

7. Squeeze some lemon juice over the soup in the Instant Pot.

8. Your dish is ready to be served.

SICILIAN VEAL POT ROAST

SERVING SIZE: 1
SERVINGS PER RECIPE: 6
FREESTYLE POINTS PER SERVING: 8
CALORIES: 220
COOKING TIME: 2 HOURS

INGREDIENTS:

Olive oil—1 teaspoon

Veal rump roast—1 kilogram

Brown onion—1, halved, thinly sliced

Carrots—2, sliced

Celery stalks—2, roughly chopped

Garlic cloves—2, thinly sliced

Dry white wine—½ cup

Diced tomatoes—400 g

Anchovies—45-g can, drained

Cinnamon stick—1

Dried chili flakes—a pinch

Currants—½ cup

Pitted black olives—½ cup

Pine nuts—2 tablespoons, toasted

Parsley leaves—fresh flat leaf

Couscous—for serving

NUTRITION INFORMATION:

    Carbohydrate—54g

    Protein—42 g

    Fat—11 g

    Sodium—681 mg

    Cholesterol—131 mg

INSTRUCTIONS:

1. In a large frying pan, put some oil and allow it to heat it over medium-high heat. Season it with salt and pepper. Put the veal in the pan and let it cook for about 8 minutes. Make sure the veal is thoroughly cooked through and browned well. Transfer everything to the Instant Pot.

2. Now adjust the heat to medium-high heat and also add celery, onion, and carrots in it. Combine it well and let it cook for about 5 minutes until the vegetables begin to turn soft.

3. Put the garlic in the Instant Pot and cook for a minute or so until fragrant. Add the wine in the Instant Pot and let it cook for about a minute. Now add the cinnamon, tomato, anchovies, and dried chili in it.

4. Season it with salt and pepper and pour the entire mixture over the veal.

5. Close the lid of the Instant Pot and allow it to cook for about 2 hours until it turns tender. Add currants all over the veal.

6. Once it is completely cooked, slice the veal and top it with olives, pine nuts, and parsley.

7. Plate it well along with couscous.

8. Your dish is ready to be served.

CARAMEL PORK WITH ASIAN GREENS

SERVING SIZE: 1
SERVINGS PER RECIPE: 6
FREESTYLE POINTS PER SERVING: 2
CALORIES: 295
COOKING TIME: 1 HOUR

INGREDIENTS:

- Pork shoulder—1 $1/5$ kilograms, boneless
- Plain flour—2 tablespoons
- Vegetable oil—2 tablespoons
- Eschalots—2, thinly sliced
- Ginger—3-cm piece, cut into thin slices
- Garlic cloves—2, thinly sliced
- Sweet chili sauce—2 tablespoons
- Chicken stock—¾ cup, Massel salt reduced
- Lime juice—2 tablespoons
- Fish sauce—1 tablespoon
- Kecap manis—¼ cup
- Kaffir lime leaves—2, finely shredded
- Steamed rice—as required
- Asian greens—as required

NUTRITION INFORMATION:

- Carbohydrate—39 g
- Protein—45 g
- Fat—23 g
- Sodium—1,013 mg
- Cholesterol—121 mg

INSTRUCTIONS:

1. Place the pork shoulder on a plate and trim off all the excess fat from it. Discard all the fat and then cut the pork shoulder into 8 pieces.

2. In a ziplock bag, add some flour and put the pork pieces in it. Sprinkle some salt and pepper in it and seal the bag. Shake the bag well to make sure the pork pieces are well coated with the flour.

3. Take a large frying pan and add some oil in it. Once the oil is heated enough, add the pork pieces in it. Let it cook for about 5 minutes and make sure it is brown from all the sides. Transfer the meat into the Instant Pot.

4. Heat the remaining oil in the pan and add ginger, garlic, and eschalots in it. Stir it well for about 3 minutes until it turns soft. Transfer everything to the Instant Pot.

5. Put the sweet chili sauce in it along with lime juice, stock, lime leaves, kecap manis, and fish sauce in the Instant Pot. Combine everything well.

6. Cover the lid of the Instant Pot and let it cook for about 6 hours on low heat. Make sure the pork turns soft and tender.

7. Remove the pork from the sauce and with the help of two forks, shred it well.

8. Plate the shredded pork along with rice and Asian greens on the plate.

9. Drizzle some of the prepared sauce all over it.

10. Your dish is ready to be served.

BEEF ROAST

SERVING SIZE: 1
SERVINGS PER RECIPE: 12
FREESTYLE POINTS PER SERVING: 3
CALORIES: 216
COOKING TIME: 25 MINUTES

INGREDIENTS:

Beef chuck roast—4 pounds, boneless

Ground cumin—1 tablespoon

Paprika—1 tablespoon

Garlic powder—2 teaspoons

Ground black pepper—1 teaspoon

Salt—½ teaspoon

Canola oil—1 tablespoon

Beef broth—¾ cup, reduced sodium

NUTRITION INFORMATION:

Carbohydrate—1 g

Protein—34 g

Fat—8 g

Sodium—210 mg

Cholesterol—67 mg

INSTRUCTIONS:

1. Place the meat on the chopping board and chop it into 8 equal pieces. Make sure you trim out all the excess fat from it.

2. In a small bowl, put some garlic powder, paprika, cumin, salt, and pepper in it.

3. Add the spice mixture all over the meat and rub the meat gently from all the sides.

4. Put oil in the Instant Pot and adjust the heat to medium-high heat.

5. Once the oil is hot, put the meat pieces in it and let it brown from all the sides. Make sure you cook in batches to let the meat cook properly.

6. Take out the meat from the Instant Pot. Set it aside.

7. Discard the excess fat from the Instant Pot and allow the meat to cool down.

8. Pour the stock in the Instant Pot and then place a trivet inside it.

9. Put the meat pieces on the trivet rack and close the lid of the Instant Pot. Allow it to cook on high heat for about 25 minutes.

10. Remove the meat from the heat and set it aside. Depressurize the Instant Pot.

11. Slice the roasted beef well. Transfer it to the plates.

12. Your dish is ready to be served.

SAFFRON CHICKEN PILAF WITH CUCUMBER SALAD

SERVING SIZE: 1
SERVINGS PER RECIPE: 4
FREESTYLE POINTS PER SERVING: 6
CALORIES: 269
COOKING TIME: 1 HOUR

INGREDIENTS:

Olive oil—2 teaspoons

Chorizo sausage—1 package, 130 g, thinly sliced

Chicken thigh cutlets—8, 1 ½ kilograms, skinless

Brown onion—1, halved, thinly sliced

Celery sticks—2, thinly sliced

Saffron threads—½ teaspoon

Chicken stock—250 ml, 1 cup

Basmati rice—200g, 1 cup, rinsed and drained

Asparagus bunch—1, trimmed ends, cut into 4 cm lengths

Lebanese cucumber—1, coarsely chopped.

Punnet cherry tomatoes—250 g, halved

Shallots—2, trimmed, thinly sliced

Fresh mint leaves—¹/₃ cup

Fresh lemon juice—2 teaspoons

NUTRITION INFORMATION:

Carbohydrate—47 g

Protein—66g

Fat—19g

Sodium—0 mg

Cholesterol—0 mg

INSTRUCTIONS:

1. Make the Instant Pot ready and add oil in it. Let it heat over medium-high heat. Put chorizo in it and allow it to cook for 3 minutes until it starts becoming crisp. Stir it occasionally. Transfer everything to a bowl.

2. Add half of the chicken in the bowl and let it cook for about 5 minutes. Turn the side of the chicken to allow it to brown on the sides.

3. Now transfer the chicken also the chorizo in the bowl. Repeat it with the remaining chicken.

4. Put onion and celery in the Instant Pot and let it cook for about 2 minutes until soft.

5. Put the chicken along with the chorizo back in the Instant Pot and add saffron in it.

6. Close the lid of the Instant Pot and let it simmer. Now adjust the heat to high and let it cook for about 10 minutes.

7. Adjust the heat again to low and cook for nearly about 25 minutes.

8. Do a natural release of pressure and open the lid of the Instant Pot.

9. Take out the chicken carefully from the Instant Pot and transfer it to bowls.

10. Add the rice in the chorizo mixture in the Instant Pot and lock its lid. Now adjust the heat to high and allow it to cook for about 5 minutes.

11. Decrease the heat to low and cook for another 3 minutes.

12. Do a natural release of pressure and remove the lid of the Instant Pot.

13. Add the asparagus in the Instant Pot and stir it well. Close the lid of the Instant Pot but make sure you do not seal it. Set everything aside for about 10 minutes until the rice is thoroughly cooked through and tender.

14. Take a bowl and put cucumber, mint, tomato, lemon juice, and shallot in it. Season it with salt and pepper.

15. Remove the chicken from the Instant Pot and take out the bones from it. Add the boneless chicken back in the pilaf.

16. Transfer everything to serving bowls. You can add some salad on the side.

17. Your dish is ready to be served.

SLOPPY JOE

SERVING SIZE: 1
SERVINGS PER RECIPE: 6
FREESTYLE POINTS PER SERVING: 2
CALORIES: 290
COOKING TIME: 20 MINUTES

INGREDIENTS:

Olive oil—1 tablespoon

Extra-lean ground beef—1 pound

Red onion—1, chopped

Green or red bell pepper—1, chopped

Carrot—1, grated

Garlic powder—2 teaspoons

Salt—1 ½ teaspoons

Water—1 cup

Chopped tomatoes—1 cup

Apple cider vinegar—¼ cup

Tomato paste—¼ cup

Worcestershire sauce—1 tablespoon

Rolled oats—½ cup

NUTRITION INFORMATION:

Carbohydrate—28 g

Protein—18 g

Fat—13 g

Sodium—670 mg

Cholesterol—45 mg

INSTRUCTIONS:

1. First of all, preheat the base of the Instant Pot. Select the Sauté mode.

2. Add olive oil in it. Put the ground beef in it and let it cook for about 5 minutes. Make sure the meat is well cooked and turns brown in color.

3. Push the beef on one side of the Instant Pot and put onion, garlic powder, carrot, and bell peppers in it. Sprinkle some salt too. Let it cook for about 5 minutes until the vegetables are completely cooked and turn soft.

4. Pour water in the Instant Pot and add the chopped tomatoes in it. Put some Worcestershire sauce, vinegar, and tomato paste in it. Combine it well. Bring the entire thing to a boil.

5. Toss the rolled oats inside the Instant Pot. Do not stir the oats in the mixture.

6. Lock the lid of the Instant Pot and seal the valve.

7. Let it cook on the Stew mode for about 10 minutes on high pressure.

8. Release the pressure of the Instant Pot through quick release.

9. Remove the lid of the Instant Pot and allow it to sit for about 5 minutes. Let the mixture thicken. Your dish is ready to be served.

CREAMY CHICKEN AND BROCCOLI PASTA

SERVING SIZE: 1
SERVINGS PER RECIPE: 4
FREESTYLE POINTS PER SERVING: 3
CALORIES: 370
COOKING TIME: 20 MINUTES

INGREDIENTS:

Olive oil—1 tablespoon, divided

Chicken breasts—1 ½ pounds, cut into cubes

Salt—1 teaspoon, divided

Ground black pepper—to taste

Broccoli—1 head

Low-fat milk—6 cups

Bow-tie pasta—1 pound

Parmesan cheese—1 cup, shredded

Mozzarella cheese—1 cup, shredded, reduced-fat

NUTRITION INFORMATION:

Carbohydrate—46 g

Protein—26 g

Fat—9 g

Sodium—510 mg

Cholesterol—50 mg

INSTRUCTIONS:

1. Take the Instant Pot and put ½ tablespoon of olive oil in it. Select the Sauté mode of the Instant Pot.

2. Put chicken in it and sprinkle ½ teaspoon of salt and pepper on it. Allow the chicken to cook for about 5–6 minutes. Cook until the chicken turns brown. Transfer the chicken into a bowl.

3. Put the remaining oil in the Instant Pot. Put the broccoli in the Instant Pot and season it with salt and pepper as desired. Cover the Instant Pot with its lid and let it cook for about 2 minutes. It should turn bright green in color.

4. Now pour the milk into the Instant Pot and allow it to boil. Keep stirring frequently. Put the pasta in it and cook for about 10 minutes. Keep stirring.

5. Add Parmesan and mozzarella cheese in the pasta. Mix well. Allow the cheese to melt. Stir in the chicken at this stage.

6. Your dish is ready to be served.

WEIGHT WATCHERS FREESTYLE DINNER RECIPES

LEMON SHRIMP AND ARTICHOKE PASTA

SERVING SIZE: 1
SERVINGS PER RECIPE: 6
FREESTYLE POINTS PER SERVING: 5
CALORIES: 404
COOKING TIME: 20 MINUTES

INGREDIENTS:

Linguine—1 pound

Parmesan cheese—$2/3$ cup, freshly grated

Lemon juice—½ cup, freshly squeezed

Extra-virgin olive oil—¼ cup

Lemon zest—1 tablespoon, grated

Unsalted butter—¼ cup

Garlic—1 ½ tablespoons, minced

Large shrimp—1 pound, peeled and deveined

Sea salt—1 teaspoon

Ground black pepper—to taste

Artichoke hearts in water—2 cans, 14 ounces, drained, pat dried, and quartered

Fresh parsley—¼ cup, minced

NUTRITION INFORMATION:

Carbohydrate—56 g

Protein—23 g

Fat—9 g

Sodium—561 mg

Cholesterol—81 mg

INSTRUCTIONS:

1. Make the Instant Pot ready and pour water in it. Put some salt in it and bring the water to a boil.

2. Add the linguine in the Instant Pot and let it cook for about 8 minutes. Reserve about a cup of water and drain out all the excess water from the Instant Pot.

3. In a large bowl, put Parmesan cheese, lemon juice, olive oil, and lemon zest in it. Mix it well.

4. Put some butter in the Instant Pot and select the Sauté mode. Once the butter has melted over medium-low heat, put some garlic in it. Make sure you sauté the garlic until fragrant.

5. Add the shrimps in it and season it with salt and pepper. Add the shrimps back in the Instant Pot and cook for about 2 minutes until it starts becoming pink in color.

6. Put the artichoke hearts and the shrimps in the Instant Pot and cook it for about 2 minutes. Stir it well.

7. In a large mixing bowl, toss the cooked pasta, artichoke hearts, shrimp, and lemon sauce together in it. Pour the reserved water in it too. Make sure you add $1/3$ cup once at a time to gain the desired consistency.

8. Garnish it with fresh parsley. Your dish is ready to be served.

POTATO SOUP

SERVING SIZE: 1
SERVINGS PER RECIPE: 5
FREESTYLE POINTS PER SERVING: 2
CALORIES: 87
COOKING TIME: 20 MINUTES

INGREDIENTS:

Butter—1 tablespoon

Bacon—2 slices, halved

Onion—½ cup, chopped

Sour cream—½ cup

Cheddar cheese—½ cup, shredded and divided

Salt—½ teaspoon

Pepper—¼ teaspoon

Green scallions—¼ cup

Russet potatoes—1 ½ pounds, peeled and diced

Chicken broth—2 cups, low sodium

NUTRITION INFORMATION:

Carbohydrate—10 g

Protein—3 g

Fat—4 g

Sodium—146 mg

Cholesterol—11 mg

INSTRUCTIONS:

1. Put the butter in the Instant Pot and press the Sauté mode. Allow the butter to melt and then add the bacon in it. Allow it to cook for about 5 minutes until crispy.

2. Take out the bacon pieces from the Instant Pot and reserve the butter and the bacon drippings.

3. Add onions in the Instant Pot and stir well. Cook for about 3 minutes until the onions turn soft and translucent.

4. Put the potatoes and the broth in it too. Lock the lid of the Instant Pot and cook for about 10 minutes on high pressure.

5. Release the pressure from the Instant Pot.

6. Take an immersion blender, pour the soup in it, and puree it until smooth.

7. Pour the sour cream in it and stir well. Add ¼ cup of cheese in it. Stir well.

8. Sprinkle some salt and pepper in it. Keep stirring until the cheese has completely melted.

9. Garnish it with crumbled bacon, green scallions, and remaining ¼ cup of the cheese.

10. Your dish is ready to be served.

HONEY-DIJON CHICKEN WITH GREEN BEANS

SERVING SIZE: 2
SERVINGS PER RECIPE: 2
FREESTYLE POINTS PER SERVING: 8
CALORIES: 235
COOKING TIME: 30 MINUTES

INGREDIENTS:

- Olive oil—2 tablespoons

- Unsalted butter—2 tablespoons, melted

- Honey—2 tablespoons

- Dijon mustard—2 tablespoons

- Garlic cloves—2, minced

- Dried oregano—½ teaspoon

- Dried basil—½ teaspoon

- Cayenne powder—$1/8$ teaspoon

- Ground black pepper—¼ teaspoon

- Kosher salt—¼ teaspoon

- Chicken breast—2, boneless and skinless

- Green beans—1 ½ cups, trimmed ends

- Lemon—1, sliced

- Vegetable oil—1 tablespoon

NUTRITION INFORMATION:

Carbohydrate—10 g

Protein—29 g

Fat—13 g

Sodium—250 mg

Cholesterol—85 mg

INSTRUCTIONS:

1. In a small bowl, put some olive oil along with melted butter, honey, mustard, garlic, oregano, basil, cayenne pepper, and black pepper in it. Sprinkle some salt in it too. Stir it well for the glaze.

2. Add vegetable oil in the Instant Pot and put the chicken in it. Add half of the glaze by brushing it all over the chicken. Now select the Sauté mode of the Instant Pot and let it cook for about 20 minutes. Make sure the chicken is thoroughly cooked through and is no longer pink in color.

3. Open the lid of the Instant Pot and put the green beans in it.

4. Sprinkle salt and pepper all over the chicken and the green beans, and add the rest of the glaze over the chicken.

5. Select the Sauté mode of the Instant Pot and let it cook for about 10 minutes. Make sure the green beans turn soft and tender.

6. Let the chicken rest for about 5 minutes.

7. Slice the chicken diagonally into ¼-inch pieces and plate it along with the green beans.

8. Your dish is ready to be served.

APRICOT LAMB WITH HONEY AND ALMOND COUSCOUS

SERVING SIZE: 1
SERVINGS PER RECIPE: 4
FREESTYLE POINTS PER SERVING: 1
CALORIES: 327
COOKING TIME: 2 HOURS

INGREDIENTS:

Olive oil—2 tablespoons

Lamb leg roast—800g, boneless

Onion—1, medium, thinly sliced

Carrots—2, halved, cut into 1-cm thick slices

Middle Eastern seasoning—2 teaspoons

Garlic cloves—2, crushed

Lemon rind—3 strips

Dried apricots—½ cup

Chicken stock—1 1/2 cups

Honey—1 tablespoon

Steamed green beans—as required

NUTRITION INFORMATION:

Carbohydrate—18g

Protein—53g

Fat—30g

Sodium—615 mg

Cholesterol—140 mg

INSTRUCTIONS:

1. In a frying pan, put oil in it and heat it over medium-high heat. Let the lamb cook for about 5 minutes or until brown in color. Transfer it in the Instant Pot.

2. Put the rest of the oil in the pan and heat it well. Put the onions and carrots in the Instant Pot and let it cook for about 3 minutes. Stir it well.

3. Season it with garlic and seasoning. Stir it again until fragrant. Transfer everything to the Instant Pot.

4. Put the lemon rind, apricots, stock, and honey in the Instant Pot and combine it well. Season it with salt and pepper as desired.

5. Close the lid of the Instant Pot and let it cook for about an hour. Make sure the lamb is thoroughly cooked through and turns tender.

6. Plate the cooked lamb on a dish and slice it well.

7. Drizzle the sauce all over the lamb and transfer it to a bowl of boiling water. Add the couscous in it. Close the lid of the Instant Pot and keep it aside for about 5 minutes. Let it set until the liquid has been absorbed properly.

8. Take two forks and fluff the grains well. Put the almonds and onions in it and season it well.

9. Combine it well.

10. Plate the lamb along with the couscous, apricot sauce, and beans in it.

11. Your dish is ready to be served.

CREAM OF MUSHROOM SOUP

SERVING SIZE: 1
SERVINGS PER RECIPE: 4
FREESTYLE POINTS PER SERVING: 7
CALORIES: 129
COOKING TIME: 20 MINUTES

INGREDIENTS:

Olive oil—1 teaspoon

Garlic cloves—2

Bay leaf—1

Peppercorns—10

Potato—1, large, roughly chopped

Mushrooms—300 g, cleaned and roughly chopped

Water—1 cup

Milk—1 cup

Salt—to taste

Olive oil—for seasoning

NUTRITION INFORMATION:

Carbohydrate—13 g

Protein—9 g

Fat—5 g

Sodium—1,777 mg

Cholesterol—9 mg

INSTRUCTIONS:

1. Make the Instant Pot ready and add the olive oil in it. Put bay leaf, pepper, corns, and garlic in it. Allow it to cook until fragrant.

2. Put the potatoes along with the mushrooms in it.

3. Add water in the Instant Pot and season it with salt as desired.

4. Close the lid of the Instant Pot and let it cook well. Do a natural release of pressure.

5. Discard the bay leaf from the Instant Pot and puree the soup with the help of a hand blender. The puree should be turned into a smooth consistency.

6. Add some milk in the Instant Pot. Season it well. Bring the entire thing to a quick boil. Turn off the heat of the Instant Pot.

7. Transfer the prepared soup into bowls. Garnish it with a dash of olive oil.

8. Your dish is ready to be served.

FRENCH-STYLE CHICKEN WITH WINTER VEGGIES AND TARRAGON

SERVING SIZE: 1
SERVINGS PER RECIPE: 4
FREESTYLE POINTS PER SERVING: 0
CALORIES: 293
COOKING TIME: 1 HOUR

INGREDIENTS:

Whole chicken—1 ½ kilograms

Extra-virgin olive oil—2 teaspoons

Leek—1, thinly sliced

Gluten-free speck—200 g, cut into batons

French shallots—6, peeled

Button mushrooms—200 g

Chicken stock—250 ml, 1 cup

White wine—½ cup

Garlic bulb—1, unpeeled and halved

Fresh tarragon—1, large sprig

Baby fennel bulbs—2, trimmed and sliced

Baby carrots bunch—1, peeled and trimmed

NUTRITION INFORMATION:

Carbohydrate—10 g

Protein—62g

Fat—43 g

Sodium—0 mg

Cholesterol—0 mg

INSTRUCTIONS:

1. Place the chicken on a plate and season it well.

2. Take the Instant Pot and set it on high heat. Select the Browning option and pour oil in it.

3. Add the chicken in the Instant Pot and cook for about 10 minutes, by turning it occasionally. Make sure the chicken is well browned from all the sides. Once the chicken is well cooked, transfer it to a plate.

4. Change the setting of the Instant Pot to Sauté mode and also adjust the heat to medium-high.

5. Now add leek, mushrooms, shallots, and specks in it. Sauté it for about 10 minutes by turning it frequently. Make sure they are well caramelized.

6. Place the chicken back in the Instant Pot on top of the speck mixture.

7. Pour the stock and wine in it and stir well. Also, add garlic and tarragon in it and lock the lid of the Instant Pot.

8. Allow it to cook on low pressure for about 30 minutes.

9. Go for a quick release of pressure and transfer the chicken on a plate. Set it aside.

10. Put the fennel and carrots in the mixture and again close the lid of the Instant Pot. Allow it to cook on low pressure for about 5 minutes. Again go for a quick release of pressure.

11. Now transfer the vegetables to the plate with the chicken. Season it well.

12. Drizzle the sauce all over the plate containing the chicken and the veggies.

13. Your dish is ready to be served.

PORK AND CAPSICUM HOTPOT

SERVING SIZE: 2
SERVINGS PER RECIPE: 8
FREESTYLE POINTS PER SERVING: 5
CALORIES: 195
COOKING TIME: 1 HOUR AND 30 MINUTES

INGREDIENTS:

Plain flour—40 g

Pork scotch fillet—1 ½ kilograms, cut into 2-cm thick slices

Olive oil—2 tablespoons

Chorizo sausage—3, cut into 1.5-cm thick slices

Red capsicums—2, halved, deseeded, and cut into 2-cm pieces

Green capsicum—1, halved, deseeded, and cut into 2-cm pieces

Red onions—2, halved and cut into wedges

Garlic cloves—3, crushed

Smoked paprika—1 teaspoon

Saffron threads—½ teaspoon

Diced tomatoes—1 can, 800g

Chicken stock—375 ml, 1 ½ cups

Cooked polenta

Fresh oregano leaves—2 tablespoons

NUTRITION INFORMATION:

Carbohydrate—13g

Protein—45 g

Fat—25 g

Sodium—0 mg

Cholesterol—0 mg

INSTRUCTIONS:

1. Take a plate and pour the flour all over it. Season it well with salt and pepper.

2. Put the pork pieces in it and toss it well to coat the meat with flour. Shake off the excess flour from the meat.

3. In the Instant Pot, add oil and heat it over medium heat. Put chorizo in it and cook it for about 2 minutes. Keep stirring occasionally or until golden brown in color. Transfer it to a plate.

4. Put the pork in the Instant Pot and cook in batches with the remaining oil.

5. Now add the onions and capsicums in the Instant Pot and stir for another 5 minutes. Put garlic, saffron, and paprika in it and cook for another minute until fragrant. Add the stock and the tomato in it.

6. In the next stage, put the chorizo and the prepared pork in it. Adjust the heat to low and let it simmer for about 30 minutes.

7. Keep the lid off the Instant Pot and let it simmer for an hour. Make sure the pork turns tender and the sauce gradually thickens.

8. Take the serving plates and serve some polenta on every plate evenly. Top it with the pork mixture and season it with oregano and salt as desired.

9. Your dish is ready to be served.

MEXICAN BEEF AND VEGETABLE STEW

SERVING SIZE: 1
SERVINGS PER RECIPE: 6
FREESTYLE POINTS PER SERVING: 4
CALORIES: 539
COOKING TIME: 1 HOUR

INGREDIENTS:

Vegetable oil—3 tablespoons, divided

Flour—¼ cup

Paprika—½ teaspoon

Salt—½ teaspoon

Pepper—¼ teaspoon

Cumin—¼ teaspoon

Mexican oregano—¼ teaspoon, dried

Garlic powder—¼ teaspoon

Beef chuck roast—2 pounds, cubed

Garlic cloves—2, crushed and minced

Diced tomatoes—2 cans, divided

Beef broth—1 quart

Bay leaves—2

Red pepper flakes—½ teaspoon, crushed

Red potatoes—3, large, quartered

Carrots—2, large, peeled and sliced

Frozen corn—2 cups

Onion—1/2, diced

Cabbage head—1/2, coarsely chopped

NUTRITION INFORMATION:

Carbohydrate—60g

Protein—28g

Fat—22g

Sodium—1,238 mg

Cholesterol—69 mg

INSTRUCTIONS:

1. Preheat the Instant Pot and put 1 tablespoon of oil in it.

2. Take a mixing bowl and add flour, salt, paprika, cumin, pepper, and oregano and garlic powder together in it. Add the cubed beef in it and coat it well in this mixture.

3. Put the beef cubes in the Instant Pot in batches and cook for about 8 minutes. Add an additional tablespoon of oil in every batch to brown the meat cubes well. Transfer it to a plate.

4. Take the Instant Pot and add minced garlic and half of the diced tomatoes in it. Scrape off the bottom of the pan. Stir well.

5. Now add the beef broth and bay leaves in the Instant Pot again. Add the cooked browned beef in the Instant Pot too. Close and lock the lid of the Instant Pot and allow it to cook for about 10 minutes.

6. Allow for natural release of pressure. Open the lid of the Instant Pot and add the other half of the diced tomatoes, quartered potatoes, corn, carrots, crushed red pepper flakes, and onion in it.

7. Lock the lid of the Instant Pot again and let it cook for another 15 minutes.

8. Once 15 minutes is over, allow for a quick release of pressure. Add the diced cabbage in the Instant Pot and lock the lid. Keep the lid closed for about 10 minutes. Allow it to rest.

9. Your dish is ready to be served.

PAN-SEARED SEA SCALLOPS IN BLACK BEAN SAUCE

SERVING SIZE: 1
SERVINGS PER RECIPE: 6
FREESTYLE POINTS PER SERVING: 7
CALORIES:125
COOKING TIME: 15 MINUTES

INGREDIENTS:

Chinese salted black beans—$1/3$ cup

Vegetable oil—2 tablespoons, divided

Scallions—4, trimmed and cut into 1-inch pieces

Sea scallops—24, large, rinsed and pat dried

Fresh ginger—1 ounce, minced

Garlic clove—1, large, minced

Shaoxing wine—$1/3$ cup

Water—$1/3$ cup

Tapioca starch/cornstarch—1 teaspoon

Water—1 teaspoon

Dark sesame oil—2 teaspoons

NUTRITION INFORMATION:

Carbohydrate—13 g

Protein—15 g

Fat—3 g

Sodium—610 mg

Cholesterol—20 mg

INSTRUCTIONS:

1. Take a small bowl and put the black beans in it. Put enough water to cover the beans. Allow it to soak for about 20 minutes. Drain the water.

2. Take the Instant Pot and put 1 tablespoon of olive oil in it. Select the Sauté mode. Let it heat on medium-high heat.

3. Put the scallions in the Instant Pot. Stir-fry for about a minute until golden brown. Keep it aside.

4. Take the Instant Pot again and put garlic and ginger in it. Stir-fry for 30 seconds until fragrant.

5. Put the black beans, $1/3$ cup of water, and wine in the skillet. Keep stirring to deglaze. Close the lid of the Instant Pot for some time and bring the liquid to a boil.

6. Once done, allow for natural release of pressure. Open the lid of the Instant Pot.

7. Take a small bowl and mix the tapioca starch along with 1 teaspoon of water. Stir well. Pour the prepared mixture over the sauce and let it cook for 30 seconds until thick. Stir well to gain a thicker consistency of the sauce.

8. Add sesame oil and stir the sauce again.

9. Take a platter and pour the sauce all over it. Assemble the scallops onto the sauce.

10. Garnish it with fried scallions.

11. Your dish is ready to be served.

CONCLUSION

Today, obesity is rising at an alarming rate where the ratio of people eating unhealthy junk food is higher than the ratio of people eating healthy food. The Weight Watchers Freestyle Instant Pot Cookbook has taken care of this common issue with a solution of cooking more than 25+ recipes in a hassle-free manner. Staying fit will ultimately help you combat multiple numbers of health problems and diseases.

Packed with detailed information about serving size, ingredients used, nutritional information, and a step-by-step guide to cook simples yet tasty using the Instant Pot, this cookbook is truly going to help you in the long run. It's time you start adopting healthy habits and a stress-free method of cooking with the all-purpose Instant Pot.

Made in the USA
Lexington, KY
29 January 2019